A Literature Kit™ FOR

Hatchet

By Gary Paulsen

Written by Sarah Joubert

GRADES 5 - 6

Classroom Complete Press
P.O. Box 19729
San Diego, CA 92159
Tel: 1-800-663-3609 | Fax: 1-800-663-3608
Email: service@classroomcompletepress.com

www.classroomcompletepress.com

ISBN – 13: 978-1-55319-557-3

 We acknowledge the financial support of the Government of Canada through the Book Publishing Industry Development Program (BPIDP) for our publishing activities. Printed in Canada.

Critical Thinking Skills

Hatchet

Level	Skills for Critical Thinking	Chapter Questions: 1	2–3	4	5	6–7	8–10	11–13	14–15	16–17	18–Epilogue	Writing Tasks	Graphic Organizers
LEVEL 1 Remembering	• Identify Story Elements	✓	✓	✓	✓	✓	✓	✓	✓	✓	✓	✓	✓
	• Recall Details	✓	✓	✓	✓	✓	✓	✓	✓	✓	✓	✓	✓
	• Match	✓	✓	✓		✓	✓	✓			✓		
	• Sequence Events		✓				✓				✓		✓
LEVEL 2 Understanding	• Compare & Contrast					✓		✓	✓	✓		✓	✓
	• Summarize	✓	✓	✓	✓	✓	✓	✓	✓	✓	✓	✓	✓
	• State Main Idea				✓	✓	✓	✓				✓	✓
	• Describe	✓	✓	✓	✓	✓	✓	✓	✓	✓	✓	✓	✓
	• Classify					✓	✓		✓		✓	✓	
LEVEL 3 Applying	• Plan			✓	✓	✓	✓	✓	✓	✓	✓	✓	✓
	• Interview											✓	
	• Infer Outcomes	✓	✓	✓	✓	✓	✓			✓			✓
LEVEL 4 Analysing	• Draw Conclusions	✓	✓	✓	✓	✓	✓	✓	✓	✓	✓	✓	✓
	• Identify Supporting Evidence	✓	✓	✓	✓	✓	✓	✓	✓	✓	✓	✓	✓
	• Motivations	✓	✓	✓	✓	✓	✓	✓	✓	✓	✓	✓	✓
	• Identify Cause & Effect						✓	✓					✓
LEVEL 5 Evaluating	• State & Defend An Opinion	✓	✓	✓	✓	✓	✓	✓	✓	✓	✓	✓	✓
	• Make Judgements	✓	✓	✓	✓	✓	✓	✓	✓	✓	✓	✓	✓
LEVEL 6 Creating	• Predict	✓	✓	✓	✓	✓		✓		✓	✓	✓	
	• Design			✓	✓	✓		✓	✓	✓	✓	✓	
	• Create			✓	✓			✓	✓	✓	✓	✓	✓
	• Imagine Alternatives		✓	✓	✓	✓	✓	✓		✓	✓	✓	

Based on Bloom's Taxonomy

Contents

Assessment Rubric

Hatchet

Student's Name: ____________________ Assignment: ______________ Level: ________

	Level 1	Level 2	Level 3	Level 4
Comprehension of Novel	Demonstrates a limited understanding of the novel	Demonstrates some understanding of the novel	Demonstrates a considerable understanding of the novel	Demonstrates a thorough understanding of the novel
Content • Information and details relevant to focus	Elements are incomplete; key details missing	Some elements are complete; details missing	All required elements are complete; key details contain some description	All required elements are complete; enough description for clarity
Style • Effective word choice and originality • Precise language	Little variety in word choice. Language vague and imprecise	Some variety in word choice. Language somewhat vague and imprecise	Good variety in word choice. Language precise and quite descriptive	Writer's voice is apparent throughout. Excellent choice of words. Precise language
Conventions • Spelling, language, capitalization, punctuation	Errors seriously interfere with the writer's purpose	Repeated errors in mechanics and usage	Some errors in convention	Few errors in convention

STRENGTHS:

WEAKNESSES:

NEXT STEPS:

Teacher Guide

Our resource has been created for ease of use by both ***TEACHERS*** *and* ***STUDENTS*** *alike.*

Introduction

Our literature kit is designed to give the teacher a number of helpful ways of making the study of this novel a more enjoyable and profitable experience for the students. Our guide features a number of useful and flexible components, from which the teacher can choose. It is not expected that all of the activities will be completed.

One advantage to this approach to the study of a novel is that the student can work at his or her own speed, and the teacher can assign activities that match the student's abilities.

Our literature kit divides the novel by chapters and features reading comprehension and vocabulary questions. Themes include survival, adapting to one's environment, family relationships, coming of age, and isolation. Hatchet provides a wealth of opportunity for classroom discussion because of its vivid portrayal of the central character, Brian, and his quest for survival that will change him for the rest of his life.

How Is Our Literature Kit™ Organized?

STUDENT HANDOUTS

Chapter Activities *(in the form of reproducible worksheets)* make up the majority of this resource. For each group of chapters, there are BEFORE YOU READ activities and AFTER YOU READ activities.

- The BEFORE YOU READ activities prepare students for reading by setting a purpose for reading. They stimulate background knowledge and experience, and guide students to make connections between what they know and what they will learn. Important concepts and vocabulary from the chapter(s) are also presented.
- The AFTER YOU READ activities check students' comprehension and extend their learning. Students are asked to give thoughtful consideration of the text through creative and evaluative short-answer questions and journal prompts.

Six **Writing Tasks** and three **Graphic Organizers** are included to further develop students' critical thinking and writing skills, and analysis of the text. *(See page 6 for suggestions on using the Graphic Organizers.)* The **Assessment Rubric** *(page 4)* is a useful tool for evaluating students' responses to the Writing Tasks and Graphic Organizers.

PICTURE CUES

This resource contains three main types of pages, each with a different purpose and use. A **Picture Cue** at the top of each page shows, at a glance, what the page is for.

Teacher Guide
- Information and tools for the teacher

Student Handout
- Reproducible worksheets and activities

Easy Marking™ Answer Key
- Answers for student activities

EASY MARKING™ ANSWER KEY

Marking students' worksheets is fast and easy with this **Answer Key**. Answers are listed in columns—just line up the column with its corresponding worksheet, as shown, and see how every question matches up with its answer!

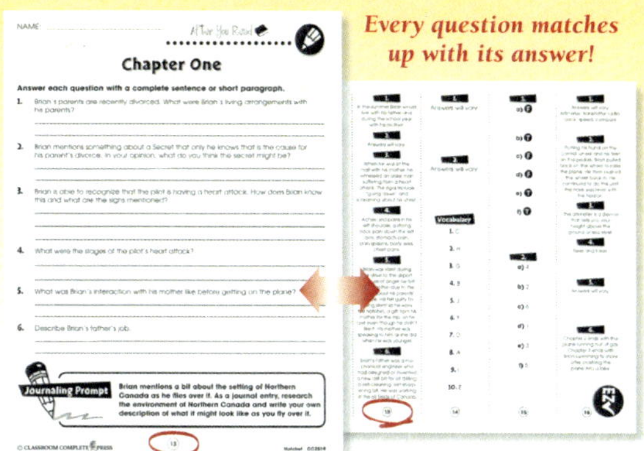

1,2,3
Graphic Organizers

The three **Graphic Organizers** included in this **Literature Kit™** are especially suited to a study of ***Hatchet***. Below are suggestions for using each organizer in your classroom, or they may also be adapted to suit the individual needs of your students. The organizers can be used on a projection system or interactive whiteboard in teacher-led activities, and/or photocopied for use as student worksheets. To evaluate students' responses to any of the organizers, you may wish to use the **Assessment Rubric** *(on page 4)*.

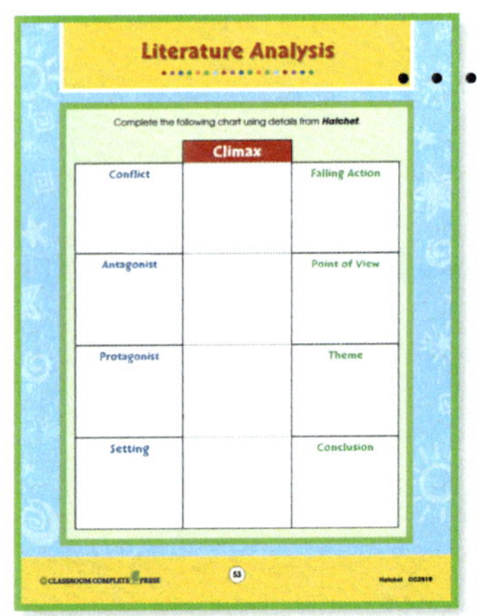

LITERATURE ANALYSIS

This activity is a culminating activity resulting from classroom discussion and questioning inherent in the study of such a novel. The teacher may choose to do this analysis with a small group of students who are ready for this activity, or as a whole group with strong direction from the teacher. Students are required to identify such critical concepts as setting, protagonist/antagonist (if it applies), conflict, climax, falling action, point of view, theme, and conclusion. It is meant to serve as an effective wrap-up in such a novel study. An enrichment activity might include a similar exercise comparing these traits with another novel with which the students are familiar. Found on Page 53.

CHARACTER DEVELOPMENT

Brian spends 54 days alone in the Canadian wilderness and he faces many difficult struggles. For each of these struggles, he learns a valuable lesson. Have the students write down the event and what they conclude Brian learned from this lesson. Found on Page 54.

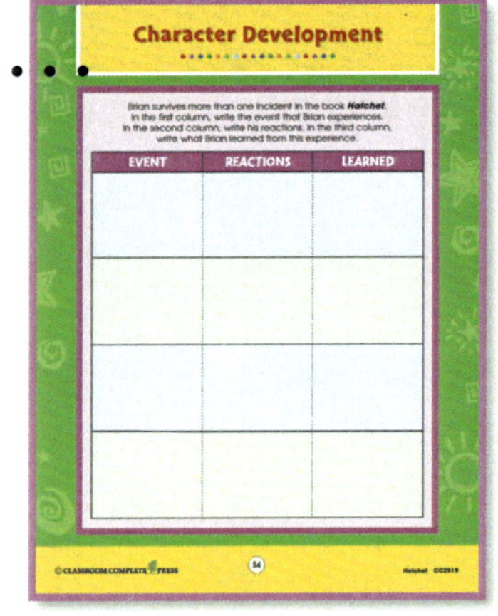

STORY MAP

Hatchet is an incredible novel dealing with themes of survival, isolation, coming of age, and being lost. Almost everything about this novel is unique: the setting (Canadian wilderness); character (Brian); the problem (being lost in the wild with only a hatchet); an intriguing plot, and unforgettable resolution. In the accompanying **Story Map**, students are asked to complete each section with details from the novel. Found on Page 55.

Bloom's Taxonomy* for Reading Comprehension

The activities in this resource engage and build the full range of thinking skills that are essential for students' reading comprehension. Based on the six levels of thinking in Bloom's Taxonomy, questions are given that challenge students to not only recall what they have read, but to move beyond this to understand the text through higher-order thinking. By using higher-order skills of applying, analyzing, evaluating and creating, students become active readers, drawing more meaning from the text, and applying and extending their learning in more sophisticated ways.

This **Literature Kit**™, therefore, is an effective tool for any Language Arts program. Whether it is used in whole or in part, or adapted to meet individual student needs, this resource provides teachers with the important questions to ask, inspiring students' interest and creativity, and promoting meaningful learning.

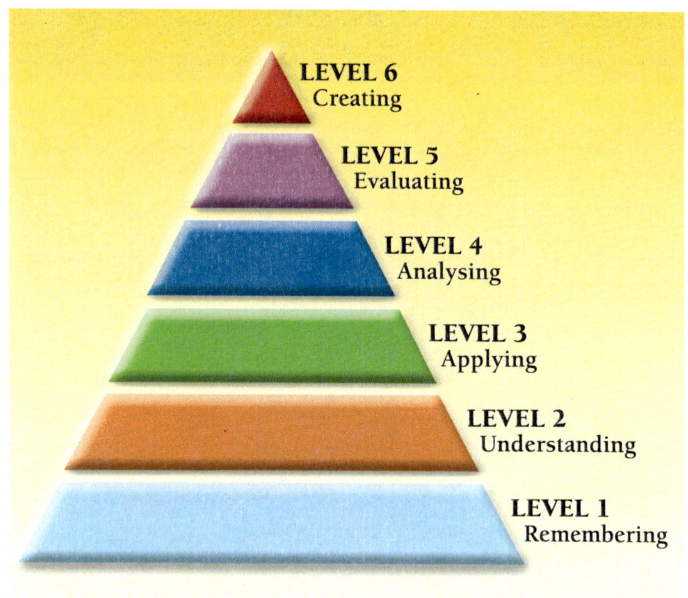

BLOOM'S TAXONOMY: 6 LEVELS OF THINKING

**Bloom's Taxonomy is a widely used tool by educators for classifying learning objectives, and is based on the work of Benjamin Bloom.*

Teaching Strategies

WHOLE-CLASS, SMALL GROUP AND INDEPENDENT STUDY

This study guide contains the following activities:

Before Reading Activities: themes are introduced and thought-provoking questions put forward for the students to consider.

Vocabulary Activities: new and unfamiliar words are introduced and reviewed.

After Reading Questions: the first part of this section includes short answer questions dealing with the content of the text. The second part features questions that are more open-ended and feature concepts from the higher order of Bloom's Taxonomy.

Writing Tasks: creative writing assignments based on Bloom's Taxonomy that relate to the plot of the particular chapters.

A comprehension quiz is also included comprised of multiple-choice, true/false and short-answer questions.

Graphic Organizers: three full-page reproducible sheets have been included and can be used for teaching purposes throughout the text.

Bonus Sheets are also available online.

The study guide can be used in a variety of ways in the classroom depending on the needs of the students and teacher. The teacher may choose to use an independent reading approach with students capable of working independently. It also works well with small groups, with most of the lessons being quite easy to follow. Finally, in other situations, teachers will choose to use it with their entire class.

Teachers may wish to have their students keep a daily reading log so that they might record their daily progress and reflections.

Summary of the Story

While on his way to visit his father in Northern Canada, thirteen-year-old Brian Robeson finds himself lost in the Canadian wilderness after the single engine plane crashes in a lake. Now, Brian is alone with only his clothing, a torn windbreaker, and the hatchet his mother gave him as a present. Brian must adapt to his environment in order to survive the mosquitoes, beavers, bears, wolves, moose, and even a tornado. While waiting for rescue, Brian must learn to fish, hunt, make a shelter, and above all, create fire. In his struggle for survival, Brian must overcome anger, self-pity, despair, loneliness, and a secret he has kept since his parents' divorce in order to survive.

Suggestions for Further Reading

OTHER BOOKS BY GARY PAULSEN

Dogsong © 1985
The Winter Room © 1989
Woodsong © 1990
The River © 1991
Brian's Winter © 1996
Brian's Return © 1999
Brian's Hunt © 2003

OTHER RECOMMENDED RESOURCES

Scott O'Dell, ***Island of the Blue Dolphins*** © 1960
Jean Craighead George, ***Julie of the Wolves*** © 1972
Barbara Smucker, ***Underground to Canada*** © 1977
Sid Fleischman, ***The Whipping Boy*** © 1987
Lois Lowry, ***Number the Stars*** © 1989
Lois Lowry, ***The Giver*** © 1993
Louise Moeri, ***Save Queen of Sheba*** © 1994

List of Vocabulary

CHAPTER 1

• bushplane • instruments • altitude • currents • drone • divorce • rudder • banked • slewed • gratitude • lurched • lashed • odor • hatchet • handgrip • stout • riveted • hokey • rethreaded • grimacing • thrumming • coma

CHAPTERS 2 TO 3

• turbulence • procedures • lurched • horizon • trembling • cowing • altimeter • depress • transmission • hesitation • propeller • hurtling • throttle • rebelled • wallow • wrenching • raked • batch • spiraling

CHAPTER 4

• hammered • grunting • hoarse • keening • scrunched • remnants • swarming • horde • desperation • agony • abating • collapse • hummocks • wincing • mound • splops • blurks

CHAPTER 5

• blister • raged • murky • teetered • trickle • stooped • stagger • frantic • amphibious • roared • asset • cawing • slewed • gradually • sloshing

CHAPTERS 6 TO 7

• diminish • glacier • pulverized • overhang • blisters • charcoal • sighing • tart • driftwood • disgust • interlaced • twinge • welted • matted • receded • ripe • crude • rotted • clusters • gorge • hind • wuffling • rustled • trotted • drenched • rivulets • seepage

CHAPTERS 8 TO 10

• musty • graves • hammered • slithering • skittered • straining • scraping • rasping • quill • segment • gestures • stiffened • scotched • ignite • tinder • kindling • sputtered • haunches • exasperation • tendrils • plucked • painstaking • smoldered • dweller • squatted • crackle • smeared • eddied • swirled • dusk • stirred • intervals • regulate • sloshing • squatted • dormant • quickened • heaped • convulse • roaringly

CHAPTERS 11 TO 13

• reburying • inwardly • snaggly • gnarled • trotted • waded • flailing • tapered • crude • hefted • thrusting • telegraphed • overripe • persistent • whine • bluff • swiveling • waggle • abrupt • flock • gutted • clouddown • extent • shafts • hummock • precise • splinters • infuriating • refracts • wiggling • swell • exulted • smeared

CHAPTERS 14 TO 15

• rectify • vital • smoldering • fragment • confines • devastating • sulfurous • corrosive • seared • slashing • impaired • thrashing • mesh • bearings • darted • enclosure • chattered • exasperated • deafening • streamlined • banded • ignited

CHAPTERS 16 TO 17

• tattered • slivers • stump • stickler • flurry • detach • muck • sputtered • hunched • pegs • downpour • bellowed • unduly • incessant • savagely • ruefully • stymied • pronounced • eddy • rivets • fuselage • shuddered • murky

CHAPTERS 18 TO EPILOGUE

• stabilizer • hack • frenzied • snarl • anchored • wheezed • substantial • eeled • wobbled • instinctive • heaving • surging • butane • sheath • antiseptic • encased • grime • frizzed • unwittingly • consumed • wiry • immensely • furor • plentiful • scarce

Gary Paulsen

Born May 17, 1939 in Minneapolis, Minnesota, **Gary Paulsen** became interested in reading at a very young age after a librarian gave him a book to read. At the age of 14, Paulsen ran away from home to join a carnival, where he acquired a taste for adventure. Paulsen first realized that he would become a writer suddenly while working as a satellite technician for an aerospace firm in California. One night, he walked off the job and never returned. Paulsen spent the next year in Hollywood as a magazine proofreader, working on his own writing at night. He then left California for a rented cabin on a lake in northern Minnesota. By the end of the winter, he had completed his first novel, The Special War. Paulsen has written more than 175 books and 200 articles and short stories for young readers. Paulsen's work features the outdoors and highlights themes such as coming of age, where the main character must master the art of survival in isolation as a rite of passage to manhood and maturity. In 1983, Paulsen entered his first Iditarod, a 1,150-mile Alaskan dog sled race, and in 1985, he completed his second. When he suffered from an attack of angina — a constriction of the airways — he was forced to give up his dogs. After a 20-year absence from dog sledding, Paulsen was scheduled to compete in the 2005 Iditarod, only to back out shortly before the start of the race. He then participated in 2006, but had to finish after only two days. Paulsen and his wife Ruth spend their time between a home in New Mexico and a house in the Pacific.

Did You Know?

- **Paulsen has had many different jobs such as an engineer, construction worker, ranch hand, truck driver, and sailor.**
- **Three of Paulsen's books, *Hatchet, Dogsong,* and *The Winter Room* are all Newbery Honor Books.**
- **The novel *Brian's Winter* is a sequel to *Hatchet*, stemming from an alternate ending.**

NAME: ______________________

Chapter One

Answer the questions in complete sentences.

1. ***Hatchet*** is a story about a boy surviving the Canadian wilderness. If you were lost in the middle of the woods, what sort of survival techniques would you encounter?

   ____

   ____

2. The story's setting is primarily the Canadian wilderness. What do you already know about this environment, including animals and terrain?

   ____

   ____

Vocabulary

Choose a word from the list that means the same or nearly the same as the underlined word. Be careful — a couple are a bit tricky!

instrument	**drone**	**banked**	**grimacing**
lurched	**lashed**	**odor**	**hatchet**

☐ **1.** Brian attached the **ax** his mother gave him to his belt.

☐ **2.** The airplane **sloped** towards the left as the pilot turned the wheel.

☐ **3.** There was a continuous **hum** coming from the rotating engine.

☐ **4.** The cargo was **fastened** securely in the rear of the plane.

☐ **5.** Mary used the supplied **device** to complete her task.

☐ **6.** The young boy was **frowning** in pain as he held his scraped knee.

☐ **7.** The passengers all **jerked** forward as the car came to a sudden stop.

☐ **8.** The garbage had to be taken out of the house due to the strong **smell** that was coming from it.

NAME: ______________________________

Chapter One

1. Put a check mark (✓) next to the answer that is most correct.

a) Brian was flying in what type of airplane while on his way to visit his dad?

- ◯ **A** A passenger airliner.
- ◯ **B** A single-engine bushplane.
- ◯ **C** A twin-engine float plane.
- ◯ **D** A helicopter.

b) Where was Brian flying from and where was he flying to?

- ◯ **A** From Hampton, New York to Northern Canada.
- ◯ **B** From New York City to Southern Canada.
- ◯ **C** From Canada to New York State.
- ◯ **D** From Hampton, New York to London, England.

c) What is Brian's father's job?

- ◯ **A** A mounted police officer.
- ◯ **B** A lumberjack.
- ◯ **C** A doctor.
- ◯ **D** A mechanical engineer.

d) What was the pilot suffering from in the airplane?

- ◯ **A** A stroke.
- ◯ **B** A sore stomach.
- ◯ **C** A heart attack.
- ◯ **D** Trouble breathing.

e) What gift did Brian's mother give him for his trip?

- ◯ **A** A hatchet.
- ◯ **B** New clothes.
- ◯ **C** A survival pack.
- ◯ **D** None of the above.

NAME: ______________________________

After You Read

Chapter One

Answer each question with a complete sentence.

1. Brian's parents are recently divorced. What were Brian's living arrangements with his parents?

2. Brian mentions something about a Secret that only he knows that is the cause for his parent's divorce. In your opinion, what do you think the secret might be?

3. Brian is able to recognize that the pilot is having a heart attack. How does Brian know this and what are the signs mentioned?

4. What were the stages of the pilot's heart attack?

5. What was Brian's interaction with his mother like before getting on the plane?

6. Describe Brian's father's job.

Brian mentions a bit about the setting of Northern Canada as he flies over it. As a journal entry, research the environment of Northern Canada and write your own description of what it might look like as you fly over it.

NAME: ______________________

Chapters Two to Three

Answer the questions in complete sentences.

1. At the end of Chapter 1, Brian is alone in the plane. What do you predict will happen to Brian in the following two chapters?

____

____

____

2. How do you think you would react in the face of an emergency similar to the one Brian is now facing?

____

____

____

Vocabulary

With a straight line, connect each word on the left with its meaning on the right.

1	**turbulence**	an instrument to determine direction	A
2	**horizon**	to search	B
3	**cowling**	violent shaking	C
4	**raked**	to move with rapid motion	D
5	**depress**	a spot of land with no trees	E
6	**batch**	a group of things	F
7	**hurtling**	a metal cover for an engine	G
8	**compass**	boundary line between earth and sky	H
9	**wallow**	to move with difficulty	I
10	**clearing**	to press down	J

NAME: ______________________________

Chapters Two to Three

1. **Circle T if the statement is TRUE or F if it is FALSE.**

T F a) Brian was able to take control of the plane immediately with no trouble.

T F b) Brian was able to use the transmitter radio, but lost the transmission.

T F c) Brian could see mountains on the horizon.

T F d) The plane crash landed in a clearing of fallen down trees.

T F e) Brian tried the radio every ten minutes while holding altitude.

T F f) The engine died between the 17th and 18th radio transmissions.

2. **Number the events from 1 to 6 in the order they occurred in these chapters.**

☐ a) Brian is able to find a lake to steer the plane to.

☐ b) Brian finds and uses the transmitter radio to call for help.

☐ c) The plane crash lands into the lake.

☐ d) Brian is left alone in the plane and takes control.

☐ e) The plane's engine dies and starts to descend.

☐ f) The plane decreases its speed and luckily heads into a clearing.

After You Read

NAME: ______________________________

Chapters Two to Three

Answer each question with a complete sentence.

1. Brian recognizes several different devices on the dashboard of the plane. Name at least 2 of them.

2. Explain how Brian first took control of the plane.

3. What is the altimeter and what does it do?

4. Describe the Canadian landscape surrounding Brian's plane.

5. At the end of Chapter 3, Brian is forced to land the plane in the lake. What would you do if you were in Brian's situation? Is there a safer alternative to landing a plane in the water?

6. The first three chapters of this book end with a cliffhanger. Describe the two cliffhangers that happen at the end of Chapter 2 and 3.

Imagine you are Brian and are faced with this life-threatening situation. Write a journal entry about your feelings and thoughts about what is happening and what you should do to ensure your survival.

NAME: ______________________________

Chapter Four

Answer the questions in complete sentences.

1. In Chapter 4, Brian reminisces about the Secret that split his parents up. What do you think the Secret is?

____

____

____

2. At the end of Chapter 3, Brian had just crashed the plane into the lake and was swimming to shore. What next obstacle do you think Brian will face in his new surroundings?

____

____

____

Vocabulary

Complete each sentence with a word from the list.

hoarse	**keening**	**remnants**	**horde**
abating	**collapse**	**hummocks**	**mound**

1. Low mounds resembling ____________ more than hills surrounded the wooded area that Brian now found himself in.

2. The funeral procession erupted in a loud ____________ cry for the lost loved one.

3. A ____________ of bicycles descended the slopping road during a cycling contest.

4. Amanda was screaming for hours that her voice became ____________.

5. Despite the massive headache Brian received from the crash, the pain in his forehead seemed to be ____________ somewhat.

6. After a long day of working in the field, Steven climbed the stairs to his bedroom in order to ____________ in his bed.

7. A small ____________ came out of the lake and a small beaver swam out of it.

8. Brian only had torn ____________ left of his windbreaker after escaping the sinking airplane and swimming to shore.

After You Read

NAME: ______________________________

Chapter Four

1. Fill in each blank with the correct word from the chapter.

a) For seconds he did not know where he was, only that the ________________ was still happening.

b) Thick, swarming hordes of ________________ that flocked to his body.

c) He couldn't identify most of it — except the evergreens — and some leafy trees he thought might be ________________.

d) It was a beaver house, called a beaver ________________.

e) The memory came in pieces — Brian looking over his head to see the ________________ and his mother sitting with the man.

2. Complete each sentence with a word from the list.

hammered	scrunched	agony	splops	blurks

a) In the end he sat with the windbreaker pulled up, almost crying in frustration and ________________.

b) He tried to move, but pain ________________ into him and made his breath shorten into gasps.

c) And if by a signal there were suddenly little ________________ all over the side of the lake.

d) Hisses and ________________, small sounds — there was great noise here, but a noise he did not know.

e) He managed to come to a sitting position and ________________ sideways until his back was against a small tree.

NAME: ______________________________

Chapter Four

Answer each question with a complete sentence.

1. What was the Secret that caused Brian's parents to divorce and how did Brian find out about it?

____

____

____

2. What temperature and time was it when Brian found out about his mother's Secret?

____

____

3. What sort of injuries did Brian sustain from the crash?

____

____

4. What did Brian believe to be "not possible"?

____

____

5. Brian describes the shape of the lake the plane crashed into as an "L" shape. At which part of the "L" did Brian swim to after the crash?

____

____

6. What types of animals, insects, and trees did Brian encounter in this chapter?

____

____

In Chapter 4, Brian wakes up on the banks of the lake alive and relatively well. Imagine you are Brian and first waking up from a plane crash. Write a journal entry describing your feelings and observations on your new environment.

NAME: ____________________

Chapter Five

Vocabulary

amphibious
Canada
cawing
frantic
hamburger
hatchet
hunger
lake
murky
North
positive
raged
slewed
teetered
trickle
yourself

Across

3. Belonging to both land and water.
6. To move unsteadily.
7. Brian was suffering from ___________.
9. "Stay ___________ and stay on top of things."
11. To turn around on its own axis.
12. Wild with fear.
15. The gift Brian's mother gave him.

Down

1. Where Brian found water to drink.
2. Where Brian was flying to visit his father.
4. Dark and gloomy.
5. What Brian's teacher said is your most valuable asset.
6. To flow or fall by drops.
8. Angry or violent.
10. What Brian couldn't stop thinking about.
13. The harsh, grating cry of the crow.
14. Where Brian had crashed.

NAME: ______________________________

Chapter Five

1. Complete the paragraph by filling in each blank with the correct word from the chapter.

They would look for him, look for the ___________ (a). His father and mother would be ___________ (b). They would tear the world apart to find him. Brian had seen searches on the news, seen movies about lost planes. When a plane went down they ___________ (c) extensive searches and almost always they found the plane within a day or two. Pilots all filed flight ___________ (d) — a detailed plan for where and when they were going to fly, with all the ___________ (e) explained. They would come, they would look for him. The ___________ (f) would get government planes and cover both sides of the flight plan filed by the pilot and search until they found him.

When the pilot pushed the ___________ (g) pedal the plane had jerked to the side and ___________ (h) a new course. Brian could not remember how much it had ___________ (i) around, but it wouldn't have had to be much because after that, Brian had ___________ (j) for hour after hour on the new course. Well away from the flight plan the pilot had filed. Many hours, at maybe ___________ (k) miles an hour. With that speed and time Brian might now be sitting several ___________ (l) miles off to the side of the recorded flight plan. They might not find him for a long time.

After You Read

NAME: ______________________________

Chapter Five

Answer each question with a complete sentence.

1. What did Brian have in his pocket?

2. Why did Brian have doubts about searchers finding him in the next day or two?

3. What was Brian hoping for after being rescued?

4. Why did Brian suddenly think of his English teacher, a man named Perpich.

5. What were the two things Brian needed to have at the end of the Chapter?

6. What happened when Brian drank water from the lake and why?

After making short-term survival plans, Brian comes to the realization that he may be several hundred miles off course of the original flight plan filed by the pilot. The searchers may not be looking for him in the right spot. Write a journal entry describing some of the long term survival plans Brian must now be thinking about.

NAME: ______________________

Chapters Six to Seven

Answer the questions in complete sentences.

1. What are the advantages for survival that Brian is exposed to in his environment?

____

____

____

2. What are the advantages for survival that Brian currently has with him?

____

____

____

____

Vocabulary

Synonyms are words with similar meanings. Use the context of the sentences below to help you choose the best synonym for the underlined word in each sentence. If you cannot determine the meaning from the context, consult a dictionary.

1. Brian's swollen forehead was already beginning to **diminish** in size.

a) enlarge **b)** reduce **c)** expand **d)** increase

2. The building was completely **pulverized** after the explosion.

a) fixed **b)** built **c)** completed **d)** destroyed

3. The old man's hairline had almost completely **receded**.

a) decreased **b)** increased **c)** advanced **d)** extended

4. The horse **trotted** over to the fence.

a) lingered **b)** ran **c)** loitered **d)** procrastinated

5. Brian felt a **twinge** in his stomach.

a) comfort **b)** relief **c)** ache **d)** pleasure

6. The baby showed his **disgust** for the broccoli by throwing it up.

a) desire **b)** appeal **c)** fondness **d)** distaste

After You Read

NAME: ______________________

Chapters Six to Seven

1. **Put a check mark (✓) next to the answer that is most correct.**

a) Where were the air force pilots placed on a survival course television show Brian saw?

◯ **A** An iceberg in Alaska.
◯ **B** A swamp in Florida.
◯ **C** A mountain in Colorado.
◯ **D** A desert in Arizona.

b) What time is it back home when the sun is high in the sky?

◯ **A** Noon
◯ **B** One or two.
◯ **C** Two or three.
◯ **D** None of the above.

c) How long did it take Brian to make a wall out of sticks and branches for his shelter?

◯ **A** 1 hour.
◯ **B** 4 hours.
◯ **C** 2 hours
◯ **D** 30 minutes.

d) What did Brian encounter when he found the raspberry patch?

◯ **A** A bear.
◯ **B** A beaver.
◯ **C** A moose.
◯ **D** A wolf.

e) What day did Brian's mother go to see the man in the station wagon?

◯ **A** Monday
◯ **B** Saturday
◯ **C** Wednesday
◯ **D** Thursday

NAME: ______________________

Chapters Six to Seven

Answer each question with a complete sentence.

1. Why did Brian want to build his shelter near the lake?

2. What were the different ways to get fire that Brian thought of?

3. What kinds of birds did Brian see?

4. How did Brian's torn windbreaker come in handy?

5. What did Brian call the berries that made him sick?

6. Describe what Brian looked like when he saw his reflection in the lake?

In Chapter 7, the author uses foreshadowing to highlight events that will come later in the story. In your journal entry, write down what you suppose the purpose of foreshadowing is in a story and why you think the author decided to include it.

NAME: ______________________

Chapters Eight to Ten

Answer the questions in complete sentences.

1. There are many dangers in the wilderness that Brian encounters, one being the bear in the previous chapter. How might Brian better protect himself from these dangers?

____

____

____

2. Think of a time when you were afraid of some hidden dangers. What did you do to protect yourself?

____

____

____

Vocabulary **Complete each sentence with a word from the list.**

slithering	**quills**	**stiffened**	**ignite**	**haunches**
exasperation	**tendrils**	**intervals**	**regulate**	**dormant**

1. The bear lay ______________ throughout the winter.

2. The porcupine stuck Brian with many of its ______________.

3. The dynamite would ______________ ten seconds after the fuse was lit.

4. The snake went ______________ by on its belly.

5. Brian found himself in ______________ after trying to make a fire all afternoon.

6. Brian had to ______________ his breathing after running through the woods.

7. A leap year happens in ______________ of 4 years.

8. The girl's hair fell like ______________ onto her shoulders.

9. The man's body ______________ in terror as he stood face to face with a bear.

10. The animal settled back on its ______________ to rest after the long run.

NAME: ___________________________

Chapters Eight to Ten

1. **Circle T if the statement is TRUE or F if it is FALSE.**

T F **a)** A turtle crawled into Brian's shelter in the middle of the night and attacked him.

T F **b)** Brian discovered fire by hitting his hatchet against the rock wall of his shelter.

T F **c)** There were 15 turtle eggs buried in the ground.

T F **d)** Brian ate 6 of the turtle eggs.

T F **e)** Brian had 8 quills stuck in his leg.

T F **f)** There were 2 white pines that were left by the windstorm where Brian got firewood from.

2. **Number the events from 1 to 6 in the order they occurred in the chapters.**

☐ **a)** Brian tries to make a fire.

☐ **b)** A porcupine attacks Brian.

☐ **c)** Brian has a hungry friend.

☐ **d)** Brian learns the most important rule of survival.

☐ **e)** Brian finds turtle eggs buried in the sand.

☐ **f)** Brian hears an animal crawl up the sand and return to the water.

After You Read

NAME: ______________________________

Chapters Eight to Ten

Answer each question with a complete sentence.

1. What was the most important rule of survival?

____

____

2. Describe how Brian made a fire.

____

____

____

3. What hungry friend did Brian make?

____

4. What did Brian discover was another advantage of having a fire?

____

____

5. Describe the turtle eggs Brian found buried in the sand.

____

____

____

6. What did the turtle eggs taste like?

____

____

In these chapters, Brian begins to understand survival. He builds a fire, finds more food, and most importantly, learns about self-worth and not feeling sorry for yourself. Pretend to be Brian and write a positive journal entry describing your most recent experiences and what you have learned about yourself.

NAME: ______________________

Chapters Eleven to Thirteen

Answer the questions in complete sentences.

1. In the coming pages, Brian begins to change from the boy he was when he crashed in the wilderness to the experienced man he will become. Describe a time when you experienced something that changed you in some way.

____

____

____

2. In the previous chapters, Brian finally managed to make a fire. How do you think this will change Brian's time in the wilderness?

____

____

____

Vocabulary

Circle the correct word that matches the meaning of the underlined word.

1. Brian moaned **inwardly** as he gathered more fire wood.

a) superficially **b)** externally **c)** outwardly **d)** within

2. The tree branches **gnarled** in a monstrous way.

a) straight **b)** unbent **c)** twisted **d)** uncurled

3. The hatchet **tapered** toward the end, making it ideal for cutting.

a) narrowed **b)** increased **c)** extended **d)** enlarged

4. The car came to an **abrupt** stop.

a) gradual **b)** sudden **c)** slow **d)** leisurely

5. A **flock** of birds flew off, surprising Brian.

a) individual **b)** single **c)** deserted **d)** group

6. Brian **exulted** in his bow and arrow and the fish he caught.

a) agonized **b)** grieved **c)** celebrated **d)** mourned

NAME: ___________________________

Chapters Eleven to Thirteen

1. Fill in each blank with the correct word from the chapters.

a) He had decided to always have enough (wood) on hand for ____________ days.

b) The lake lay before him, ____________ or so feet below.

c) The ____________ claimed all that was below him as his own.

d) Forty-two days had passed since Brian had died and been born as ____________.

e) A persistent ____________ was in his ears and he chopped and cut and was thinking of a bow and still the sound did not cut through until the ____________ was nearly off the tree.

2. Complete each sentence with a word from the list.

mistakes	refracts	kingfisher	feast	invent

a) Brian saw a ____________, described as blue with a crest and sharp beak.

b) After his fish spear didn't work, Brian had to ____________ the bow and arrow.

c) Brian had made a lot of ____________.

d) He forgot that water ____________, bending light.

e) After Brian finally caught his first fish, he had a ____________, eating over twenty of them.

NAME: ______________________

Chapters Eleven to Thirteen

Answer each question with a complete sentence.

1. How was Brian's body changing in Chapter 11?

2. Describe the bird Brian saw "explode" from under his feet.

3. Why did Brian drop everything to run back to his camp in order to light a signal fire?

4. What are food fish?

5. What "two true things" changed Brian and how?

6. What did Brian have hope for other than to be rescued?

Brian's time in the Canadian wilderness was changing not only his physical appearance, but changing his mind as well. He was becoming much more aware and knowledgeable of his environment. Imagine you are Brian at this moment and write a journal entry describing your experiences so far and how it has changed you, both physically and mentally.

NAME: ____________________

Chapters Fourteen to Fifteen

Answer the questions in complete sentences.

1. Brian quickly learns that food and shelter are the two most important things to survive in nature. How does this relate to your everyday life? What are other things that are important for survival?

____

____

2. What are some strategies you would have for hunting food and creating shelter in nature?

____

____

Vocabulary **Write a complete sentence using the following words. Make sure that the meaning of each word is clear in your sentence.**

Smoldering ______________________________

____

Confines ______________________________

____

Corrosive ______________________________

____

Enclosure ______________________________

____

Exasperated ______________________________

____

Ignited ______________________________

____

Deafening ______________________________

____

NAME: ______________________

After You Read

Chapters Fourteen to Fifteen

1. Complete the paragraph by filling in each blank with the correct word from the chapters.

On the day of ______ (a) he had decided the best thing to try for would be a ______ (b) and that morning he had set out with his bow and ______ (c) to get one. The morning sun had cooked him until it seemed his brain was ______ (d), sitting by the tree, but nothing came until he got up and started to walk again and hadn't gone two steps when a bird got up. It had been there all the time, while he was thinking about how to ______ (e) them. But this time, when the bird ______ (f), something caught his eye and it was the secret ______ (g). The bird cut down toward the ______ (h), then, seeing it couldn't land in the ______ (i), turned and flew back up the hill into the ______ (j). When it turned, curving through the trees, the sun had caught it, and Brian, for an instant,.saw it as a shape; ______ (k) in the front, back from the head in a streamlined ______ (l) shape to the fat body. Kind of like a ______ (m), he had thought, with a point on one end and a fat little body. And that had been the secret. He had been looking for ______ (n), for the color of the bird. He had to look for the ______ (o) instead, had to see the shape instead.

2. Choose the most appropriate answer for each of the following:

a) What took the rest of Brian's turtle eggs?

- ◯ **A** Beaver.
- ◯ **B** Skunk.
- ◯ **C** Bear.
- ◯ **D** Porcupine.

b) How long did it take Brian to build his new shelter?

- ◯ **A** 1 day.
- ◯ **B** 2 days.
- ◯ **C** 3 days.
- ◯ **D** 4 days.

c) What big event did Brian remember?

- ◯ **A** The day of first fish.
- ◯ **B** The day of first fire.
- ◯ **C** The day of first shelter.
- ◯ **D** The day of first meat.

d) What small animal did Brian NOT see while looking for wood?

- ◯ **A** Rabbits.
- ◯ **B** Squirrels.
- ◯ **C** Skunks.
- ◯ **D** Foolbirds.

After You Read

NAME: ______________________

Chapters Fourteen to Fifteen

Answer each question with a complete sentence.

1. What did Brian learn was the most important thing, the vital knowledge that drives all creatures in the forest?

2. Why would the skunk attack be considered one of the most devastating mistakes Brian made?

3. Describe how Brian improved his shelter.

4. How did Brian solve his food storage problem?

5. How did Brian store live fish?

6. How did Brian keep track of the days that passed?

In chapter 15, Brian discovers the "secret key" to seeing the "foolbirds" who easily blend into their environment. Do some research into other animals that blend into their surroundings. In a journal entry, explain why this technique is beneficial to these animals in the wild. Then, imagine you are Brian and write a journal entry describing strategies you would take to hunting them in the environment they are found in.

NAME: ___________________________

Chapters Sixteen to Seventeen

Answer the questions in complete sentences.

1. In the previous chapters, Brian had become a better hunter, improved his shelter, and solved his food storage problem. What are some other survival techniques Brian will face?

____

____

____

2. In the upcoming chapters, Brian faces new predators and weather conditions. How might he prepare himself for unseen hardships?

____

____

____

Vocabulary

In each of the following sets of words, underline the one word which does not belong. Then write a sentence explaining why it does not fit.

1. **a)** glided **b)** sputtered **c)** stumbled **d)** falter

____

2. **a)** bent **b)** cowered **c)** hunched **d)** straightened

____

3. **a)** cruelly **b)** savagely **c)** gently **d)** wildly

____

4. **a)** assured **b)** vague **c)** noticeable **d)** pronounced

____

5. **a)** murky **b)** smoky **c)** clear **d)** muddy

____

NAME: ______________________________

Chapters Sixteen to Seventeen

1. Put a check mark (✓) next to the answer that is most correct.

a) Which of the following is NOT a day of firsts Brian celebrated?

- ◯ **A** Day of First Meat.
- ◯ **B** First Arrow Day.
- ◯ **C** First Rabbit Day.
- ◯ **D** Day of First Fish.

b) How many arrows did it take Brian to finally hit a foolbird?

- ◯ **A** Two
- ◯ **B** Three
- ◯ **C** Four
- ◯ **D** Five

c) Brian gets savagely attacked by what animal?

- ◯ **A** A moose.
- ◯ **B** A bear.
- ◯ **C** A skunk.
- ◯ **D** A deer.

d) What woke up Brian?

- ◯ **A** A moose.
- ◯ **B** A skunk.
- ◯ **C** A tornado.
- ◯ **D** A porcupine.

e) What did the tornado bring out of the lake?

- ◯ **A** His fish gate.
- ◯ **B** The tail of the plane.
- ◯ **C** The beaver dam.
- ◯ **D** A fallen tree log.

NAME: ______________________________

Chapters Sixteen to Seventeen

Answer each question with a complete sentence.

1. Describe the method Brian perfected to hunt foolbirds.

2. What injuries did Brian receive during the moose attack?

3. What was Brian grateful for after the moose attack?

4. What did the wind from the tornado throw out into the lake?

5. What was the plane project, and what was Brian's plan for it?

6. Why did Brian have a hard time making a raft and how did he fix it?

At the end of Chapter 17, Brian manages to reach the plane on his raft. He is now faced with a new problem: getting into the tail of the plane. Imagine you are Brian and think up ways to get inside the tail of the plane. Then, predict how Brian will accomplish this in the following chapters.

NAME: ______________________

Chapters Eighteen to Epilogue

Answer the questions in complete sentences.

1. In the last chapter, Brian was contemplating how to safely get access to the tail of the plane. Make a prediction of how he will accomplish this.

____

____

____

2. We are nearing the end of the book. Make a prediction whether you think Brian will be rescued or not and how.

____

____

____

Vocabulary

Choose a word from the list that means the same as the underlined word.

frenzied	**heaving**	**surging**	**antiseptic**
consumed	**immensely**	**plentiful**	**scarce**

[ ] **1.** The amount of apples picked off the tree was **abundant**.

[ ] **2.** The stream was **flowing** with small fish.

[ ] **3.** The crowd was **frantic** with excitement as the band entered the stage.

[ ] **4.** Brian had a **limited** supply of arrows when he went out hunting.

[ ] **5.** The 10 mile run **drained** the rest of the runner's energy.

[ ] **6.** The survival pack was **jam-packed** with food and supplies.

[ ] **7.** Jake's mom cleaned his scrape with **sterile** wipes before putting on the band-aid.

[ ] **8.** Brian was **extremely** grateful for the pilot who found him.

NAME: ______________________________

Chapters Eighteen to Epilogue

1. Circle T if the statement is TRUE or F if it is FALSE.

T F **a)** Brian dove 3 times into the lake water to retrieve his hatchet.

T F **b)** Brian realized the fish he was eating had been eating the pilot's head.

T F **c)** Brian found a radio in the survival pack so he could call for help.

T F **d)** Brian ate a four-person beef and potato dinner with orange drink and peach whip for his feast.

T F **e)** Brian was surprised by the arrival of the plane while cooking his feast.

T F **f)** Three months had passed since "they" stopped searching for Brian.

2. Number the events from 1 to 6 in the order they occurred in the chapters.

☐ **a)** Brian retrieved the survival kit from the plane.

☐ **b)** Brian cooks a feast.

☐ **c)** A fur buyer flies into Brian's camp.

☐ **d)** Brian dropped the hatchet into the lake.

☐ **e)** Brian was alone on the L-shaped lake for 54 days.

☐ **f)** Brian fell asleep on the beach.

After You Read

NAME: ______________________

Chapters Eighteen to Epilogue

Answer each question with a complete sentence.

1. How did Brian gain access to the tail of the plane?

2. Why might it be important for Brian not to throw anything away?

3. What was included in the food packets in the survival pack?

4. What instructions came with the food packets?

5. What did Brian say to the pilot?

6. What changes were permanent for Brian?

It must have been a strange sight when the pilot found Brian among his shelter cooking dinner. In your final journal entry, write your reaction from either the pilot's or Brian's point of view.

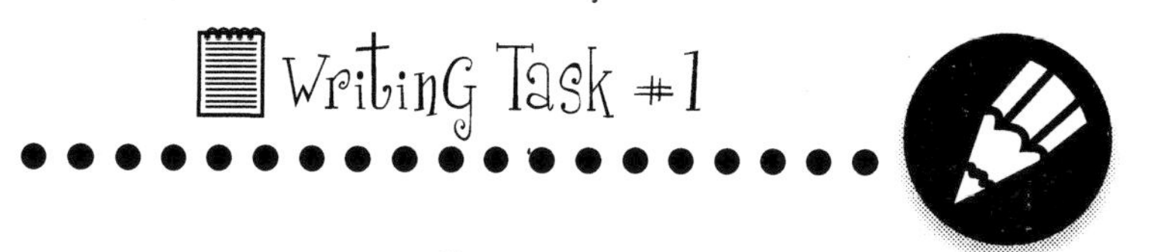

Chapters 1 to 6

Cover Art

The cover image of a book is meant to capture the attention of the reader while also depicting something important about the story, such as the main character, setting, or theme of the story.

Draw your own cover art for the novel, ***Hatchet***. Make sure to include something important to the story while still capturing the attention of the reader.

Be sure to include the title and author on your cover as well.

Chapter 7

Foreshadowing

Foreshadowing is a literary device employed by the author to give a hint that something is coming up in the story, "How was I to know that I would be in for the adventure of a lifetime." Chapter 7 may contain an example of foreshadowing: when Brian comes across an open field where the trees have all been torn up out of the ground, he says *"There must have been fierce winds to tear up places like this."*

How could this be interpreted as an example of foreshadowing?

If it is an example of this literary device, what do you think it might be predicting?

Do you think foreshadowing is a useful literary device, or would you rather the author not include this? Explain your answer.

Chapters 8 to 10

A Comic Strip

This activity is especially for students with an artistic flair or who love comic books! It can be done for events described so far in ***Hatchet***, or included in Chapters 8–10.

The first step is to decide on the length of your comic strip (6–12 frames is suggested); next, consider what events you will include. You may wish to highlight a brief incident or encompass the highlights of a chapter — or even the first 10 chapters. You may even want to provide an alternate ending to your scene!

A quick sketch of the comic strip can first be accomplished in a **storyboard format** before a final, good copy is attempted. The strip should include a title, dialogue, and color. It should be neat and imaginative.

Chapters 11 to 15

Drawing the Scene

Brian's shelter improves throughout the course of the book; however, the location remains the same.

Brian describes his shelter and surrounding location in great detail. In Chapter 6, Brian describes the location of his shelter as:

- On the northern side of the ridge, a glacier scooped part of it, leaving a sideways bowl under a ledge.
- Not as deep as a cave, it had a roof and a small sand beach that went down to the edge of the water.

In Chapter 14, Brian describes the improvements he made on his shelter:

- First he tore down his old shelter, fastened several logs from dead pines across the opening, wedging them at the top and burying the bottoms in the sand.
- He wove long branches in through them to make tighter walls.
- He weaved a door of willows in a tight mesh, and arranged some cut-off limbs to hook the door in place.

Draw Brian's shelter and location. Be sure to include the lake and improved shelter he made.

Chapters 16 to 17

The Interview

This activity is to be done in pairs.

This is your opportunity to find out what your classmates think about the novel, Hatchet, thus far in your reading.

Pair up with another student in your class who is reading the novel. Each of you will interview the other to find out his or her feelings about the experience thus far.

Prepare a list of four questions to ask your partner. The questions could involve an incident in the story itself or you may ask them what their favorite scene of the story is. Try to come up with five questions.

After asking the questions and recording your partner's answers, then it is your turn to answer your partner's questions about the novel. It is important that you give thought to each of your responses, and make them as interesting as possible.

Chapters 18 to Epilogue

Worth Posting!

Your assignment is to write a brief review of ***Hatchet*** for posting on a website such as www.amazon.com. This is an opportunity to share your opinion of the novel with other young readers who are considering whether to read the book or not.

Your review should be at least two paragraphs in length. One paragraph should briefly describe the plot (without giving away the ending). The second paragraph should give your impression of the novel.

When writing your impression, try to include one favorable comment and one suggestion as to how the novel might be improved.

NAME: ______________________________

Word Search Puzzle

Find the following words from the story. The words are written horizontally, vertically, diagonally, and some are written backwards.

bear	**bushplane**	**hatchet**	**porcupine**	**survival pack**
beaver	**divorce**	**moose**	**shelter**	**tornado**
birchbark	**fire**	**mosquitoes**	**skunk**	**turbulence**
bow and arrow	**foolbirds**	**pilot**	**spear**	**windbreaker**

b	i	r	c	h	b	a	r	k	q	u	p	s	s
u	o	m	s	u	p	v	l	d	z	l	i	e	u
s	o	w	u	x	e	r	i	f	b	o	l	o	r
h	r	f	a	f	a	d	t	e	e	d	o	t	v
p	s	y	v	n	i	h	n	s	a	p	t	i	i
l	u	b	b	o	d	i	v	o	r	c	e	u	v
a	t	e	h	c	t	a	h	l	y	r	s	q	a
n	i	a	o	s	e	r	r	u	q	v	l	s	l
e	w	v	e	o	d	a	n	r	o	t	n	o	p
s	c	e	t	r	m	e	s	o	o	m	u	m	a
t	u	r	b	u	l	e	n	c	e	w	p	s	c
s	h	e	l	t	e	r	r	l	k	u	a	t	k
k	k	u	a	s	d	r	i	b	l	o	o	f	i
u	l	o	p	o	r	c	u	p	i	n	e	p	l
n	r	e	l	w	d	b	i	r	v	e	b	m	m
k	a	g	u	p	y	t	r	s	m	o	f	l	w
r	e	k	a	e	r	b	d	n	i	w	s	u	v

NAME: ______________________

Comprehension Quiz

Answer each question in a complete sentence.

1. Why did Brian want to build his shelter near the lake?

2. Describe the location of Brian's shelter.

3. Describe the dream Brian had in Chapter 8.

4. Name TWO animals that attacked Brian.

5. What did Brian discover was another advantage of having a fire?

6. Describe what the turtle eggs looked and tasted like.

7. What did Brian have hope for other than to be rescued?

SUBTOTAL: /13

NAME: ______________________________

Comprehension Quiz

8. Name TWO "Day of Firsts" that Brian had. (2)

9. Describe Brian's method to hunting foolbirds. (3)

10. What injuries did Brian receive during the moose attack? (2)

11. What was the "plane project"? (1)

12. What problems did Brian face when trying to get the raft to the plane, and how did he resolve them? (4)

13. Why might it be important for Brian not to throw anything away? (2)

14. Name THREE things Brian found in the survival pack. (3)

SUBTOTAL: /17

11

1. Answers will vary.

2. Answers will vary.

Vocabulary

1. hatchet

2. banked

3. drone

4. lashed

5. instrument

6. grimacing

7. lurched

8. odor

12

1.

a) ✓ B

b) ✓ A

c) ✓ D

d) ✓ C

e) ✓ A

13

1. In the summer Brian would live with his father and during the school year with his mother.

2. Answers will vary.

3. When he was at the mall with his mother, he witnessed an older man suffering from a heart attack. The signs include "going down" and screaming about his chest.

4. Aches and pains in his left shoulder, a strong odor, pain down the left arm, stomach pain, pain spasms, body jerks, chest pains.

5. Brian was silent during the drive to the airport because of anger he felt for his mother due to the Secret about his parents' divorce. He felt guilty for being silent so he wore the hatchet, a gift from his mother for the trip, on his belt even though he didn't like it. His mother was speaking to him as she did when he was younger.

6. Brian's father was a mechanical engineer who had designed or invented a new drill bit for oil drilling: a self-cleaning, self-sharpening bit. He was working in the oil fields of Canada.

14

1. Answers will vary.

2. Answers will vary.

Vocabulary

1. C

2. H

3. G

4. B

5. J

6. F

7. D

8. A

9. I

10. E

15

1.

a) F

b) T

c) F

d) F

e) T

f) T

2.

a) 4

b) 2

c) 6

d) 1

e) 3

f) 5

16

1. Answers will vary. Altimeter, transmitter radio, clock, speed, compass.

2. Putting his hand on the control wheel and his feet on the pedals, Brian pulled back on the wheel to raise the plane. He then pushed the wheel back in. He continued to do this until the nose was level with the horizon.

3. The altimeter is a device that tells you your height above the ground or sea level.

4. Trees and lakes.

5. Answers will vary.

6. Chapter 2 ends with the plane running out of gas. Chapter 3 ends with Brian swimming to shore after crashing the plane into a lake.

EZ✓

1.
Answers will vary.

2.
Answers will vary.

Vocabulary

1. hummocks
2. keening
3. horde
4. hoarse
5. abating
6. collapse
7. mound
8. remnants

1.
a) crash
b) mosquitoes
c) aspen
d) lodge
e) station wagon

2.
a) agony
b) hammered
c) splops
d) blurks
e) scrunched

1.
Brian's mother was seeing another man. Brian saw her in his station wagon while riding his bike by the mall.

2.
The temperature was 82°F and it was 3:31 p.m.

3.
Sharp pains and dull aches; leg, forehead and back pains; cramped legs; throbbing head; swollen forehead; but nothing broken.

4.
The swarming hordes of mosquitoes that flocked to his body, made a living coat on his skin, clogging his nostrils and pouring into his mouth.

5.
At the base of the "L", looking up the long part with the short part out to his right.

6.
Mosquitoes, small black flies, a large bird that looked like a crow, pines, spruce, evergreens, aspen, beavers, and fish.

Vocabulary

Across
3. amphibious
6. teetered
7. hunger
9. positive
11. slewed
12. frantic
15. hatchet

Down
1. lake
2. North
4. murky
5. yourself
6. trickle
8. raged
10. hamburger
13. cawing
14. Canada

1.
a) plane
b) frantic
c) mounted
d) plans
e) courses
f) searchers
g) rudder
h) assumed; **i)** pulled
j) flown
k) 160
l) hundred

EZ✓

1.
A quarter, three dimes, a nickel, two pennies, a finger-nail clipper, a billfold with a twenty-dollar bill, and some odd pieces of paper.

2.
When the pilot had his heart attack, he pushed on the rudder pedal and the plane had jerked to the side and assumed a new course away from the flight plan, so searchers will be looking for him in the wrong place.

3.
A large, cheesy, juicy burger with tomatoes and double fries with ketchup and a thick chocolate shake.

4.
Perpich always talked about being positive, thinking positive, and staying on top of things. Thinking of Perpich motivated Brian to think about what he has that will help him to survive and to stay positive.

5.
He had to have some kind of shelter and he had to have something to eat.

6.
He immediately got sick and threw up most of the water. This most likely happened because he drank too much of the murky water too fast.

Page 23

1. Answers will vary.

2. Answers will vary.

Vocabulary

1. b

2. d

3. a

4. b

5. c

6. d

Page 24

1.

a) D

b) B

c) C

d) A

e) D

Page 25

1. Because he thought the plane might show up to somebody flying over and he didn't want to diminish any chance he might have of being found.

2. Matches, a watch crystal as a magnifying glass to focus the sun, rub two sticks together.

3. A robin, sparrows, a flock of reddish orange birds with thick beaks.

4. He used it as a carrying pouch to collect and transport the berries he found.

5. Gut cherries.

6. Face cut and bleeding, swollen and lumpy, the hair all matted, a healed cut on his forehead, covered with dirt and bites.

Page 26

1. Answers will vary.

2. Answers will vary.

Vocabulary

1. dormant

2. quills

3. ignite

4. slithering

5. exasperation

6. regulate

7. intervals

8. tendrils

9. stiffened

10. haunches

Page 27

1.

a) F

b) T

c) F

d) T

e) T

f) F

2.

a) 3

b) 1

c) 4

d) 2

e) 6

f) 5

Page 28

1. Feeling sorry for yourself didn't work.

2. First he made kindling out of thinly sliced birchbark, then he struck the black rock with the back of the hatchet, sending sparks into the kindling. Finally, he gently blew air into the growing sparks until a fire erupted.

3. The fire.

4. The smoke kept the mosquitoes away.

5. Almost perfectly round, the size of table tennis balls. White, leathery shells that gave instead of breaking when he squeezed them.

6. It had a greasy, almost oily taste.

EZ✓

EZ✓

1.
Answers will vary.

2.
Answers will vary.

Vocabulary

1. d

2. c

3. a

4. b

5. d

6. c

(29)

1.
a) three

b)twenty

c) wolf

d) the new Brian

e) whine, limb

2.
a) kingfisher

b) invent

c) mistakes

d) refracts

e) feast

(30)

1.
He lost all the extra weight he had just above his belt at the sides. His stomach had caved in to the hunger and the sun had tanned his skin. The smoke from the fire was starting to make his face look like leather.

2.
Speckled, brown and gray.

3.
Because he heard a plane approaching.

4.
Food fish stayed close in the shallows and made quick, small movements.

5.
The plane passing over him and that he would not die. The disappointment he felt when the plane passed over him cut him down and made him new. Also, he would not let death in again.

6.
Hope in his knowledge that he could learn and survive and take care of himself.

(31)

1.
Answers will vary.

2.
Answers will vary.

Vocabulary
Answers will vary.

(32)

1.
a) First Meat; **b)** foolbird **c)** spear

d) frying

e) see; **f)** flew

g) key; **h)** lake

i) water; **j)** trees

k) sharp-pointed; **l)** bullet **m)** pear

n) feathers

o) outline

2.
a) ✓ B ✓ **b)** C

c) ✓ D ✓ **d)** C

(33)

1.
Food is everything. It was the great, single driving influence in nature.

2.
The skunk's spray rendered Brian blind for almost two hours, the pain in his eyes lasted for days, and bothered him for two weeks. The smell lingered for almost a month and a half later.

3.
First he tore it down, fastened several logs from dead pines across the opening, wedging them at the top and burying the bottoms in the sand. He wove long branches in through them to make tighter walls. He weaved a door of willows in a tight mesh, and arranged some cut-off limbs to hook the door in place.

4.
There was a small ledge about 10 feet up the rock face above his shelter door that would be unreachable by small animals. In order for Brian to reach it, he made a ladder out of a dead pine tree with small branches sticking out of it.

5.
He trapped them in a large pen made of rocks and lured them with old fish waste as food. Once enclosed in the pen, Brian made a gate by weaving small willows together into a fine mesh and closed them in.

6.
He made a mark for each day in stone near the door to his shelter.

(34)

1. Answers will vary.

2. Answers will vary.

Vocabulary

Reasons will vary.

1. a

2. d

3. c

4. b

5. c

35

1.

a) ✓ D

b) ✓ B

c) ✓ A

d) ✓ C

e) ✓ B

36

---

1. When he spots a bird, he approaches it at an angle so that it seems he is moving off to the side. He never looks at the bird directly, and pauses when the bird's head feathers come up, a sign that the bird is about to fly away. When the bird becomes calm again, Brian continues.

2. Ribs were hurt bad, he could only take short breaths, and pain in his right shoulder.

3. He was grateful that the coals from the fire were still glowing; that he had thought to get wood first thing in the mornings; that he had thought to get enough wood for two or three days at a time; that he had fish nearby if he needed to eat; and that he was alive.

4. The shelter wall, bed, fire and tools.

5. The plane project was to somehow get the survival kit out of the tail of the plane that was now sticking out of the lake. Brian's plan for it was to make a raft and push-paddle it to the plane and tie it there to make a working base so he could rip or cut his way into the tail of the plane.

6. He had no rope, crosspieces or nails to keep the logs together. He fixed the problem by using logs with branches still attached.

37

---

1. Answers will vary.

2. Answers will vary.

Vocabulary

1. plentiful

2. surging

3. frenzied

4. scarce

5. consumed

6. heaving

7. antiseptic

8. immensely

38

1.

a) F

b) T

c) F

d) T

e) T

f) F

2.

a) 2

b) 4

c) 5

d) 1

e) 6

f) 3

39

---

1. After hitting the tail of the plane with his fist in frustration, he noticed the aluminum covering gave easily under his blow. Using the hatchet, he hacked his way through the plane as easily as cutting through soft cheese.

2. Answers may vary. They might be useful later, such as bits of metal from the plane could be used as fish arrowheads or lures.

3. Freeze-dried beef dinner with potatoes, cheese and noodle dinners, chicken dinners, egg and potato breakfasts, fruit mixes, drink mixes, dessert mixes.

4. Just add water, cook for half an hour or until everything was normal-size and done.

5. "My name is Brian Robeson. Would you like something to eat?"

6. Gained the ability to observe what was happening and react to it. He had become more thoughtful as well, thinking slowly about something before speaking.

EZ✓

40

Word Search Puzzle

b	i	r	c	h	b	a	r	k	q	u	p	s	s
u	o	m	s	u	p	v	l	d	z	l	i	e	u
s	o	w	u	x	e	r	i	f	b	o	l	o	r
h	r	f	a	f	a	d	t	e	e	d	o	t	v
p	s	y	v	n	i	h	n	s	a	p	t	i	i
l	u	b	b	o	d	i	v	o	r	c	e	u	v
a	t	e	h	c	t	a	h	l	y	r	s	q	a
n	i	a	o	s	e	r	r	u	q	v	l	s	l
e	w	v	e	o	d	a	n	r	o	t	n	o	p
s	c	e	t	r	m	e	s	o	o	m	u	m	a
t	u	r	b	u	l	e	n	c	e	w	p	s	c
s	h	e	l	t	e	r	r	l	k	u	a	t	k
k	k	u	a	s	d	r	i	b	l	o	o	f	i
u	l	o	p	o	r	c	u	p	i	n	e	p	l
n	r	e	l	w	d	b	i	r	v	e	b	m	m
k	a	g	u	p	y	t	r	s	m	o	f	l	w
r	e	k	a	e	r	b	d	n	i	w	s	u	v

1. Because he thought the plane might show up to somebody flying over.

2. On the northern side of the ridge, a glacier scooped part of it, leaving a sideways bowl under a ledge. Not as deep as a cave, it had a roof and a small sand beach that went down to the edge of the water.

3. His father standing at the side of a living room, trying to tell Brian something. His mouth moved, but no noise came out. His father faded into a fog and was replaced by his friend Terry. Terry was sitting in the park at a bench looking at a barbecue pit, then started a fire and pointed at it while looking at Brian.

4. Two of: porcupine, skunk, moose.

5. The smoke kept the mosquitoes away.

6. Almost perfectly round, the size of table tennis balls. White, leathery shells that gave instead of breaking when he squeezed them. They had a greasy, almost oily taste.

7. Hope in his knowledge that he could learn and survive and take care of himself.

8. Two of: Day of First Meat, Day of First Arrow, Day of First Rabbit.

9. When he spotted a bird, he approached it at an angle so that it seemed he was moving off to the side. He paused when the bird's head feathers came up. When the bird became calm again, Brian would continue.

10. Ribs were hurt bad, he could only take short breaths, and pain in his right shoulder.

11. To somehow get the survival kit out of the tail of the plane that was now sticking out of the water.

12. First he realized he had nothing to tie the raft to the plane. He tore up thin pieces from his windbreaker to make a rope. Next, the branches sticking out of the logs dragged in the water making it impossible for Brian to reach the plane before dark. He decided to turn back and start early the next morning.

13. Answers may vary. They might be useful later, such as bits of metal from the plane could be used as fish arrowheads or lures.

14. Three of: sleeping bag, foam sleeping pad, an aluminum cook set, cutlery, a waterproof container with matches and two small butane lighters, a sheath knife, a first-aid kit, a cap that said CESSNA across the front, a fishing kit, a survival rifle, two bars of soap, food packets and a small electronic device encased in a plastic bag.

Literature Analysis

Complete the following chart using details from ***Hatchet***.

Conflict	Climax	Falling Action
Antagonist		Point of View
Protagonist		Theme
Setting		Conclusion

Character Development

Brian survives more than one incident in the book ***Hatchet***. In the first column, write the event that Brian experiences. In the second column, write his reactions. In the third column, write what Brian learned from this experience.

EVENT	REACTIONS	LEARNED

Story Map

Complete each section with the appropriate details.
Setting (Time and Place):
Characters
Major:
Minor:
Problem/Challenge:
Plot/Key Events:
Resolution:

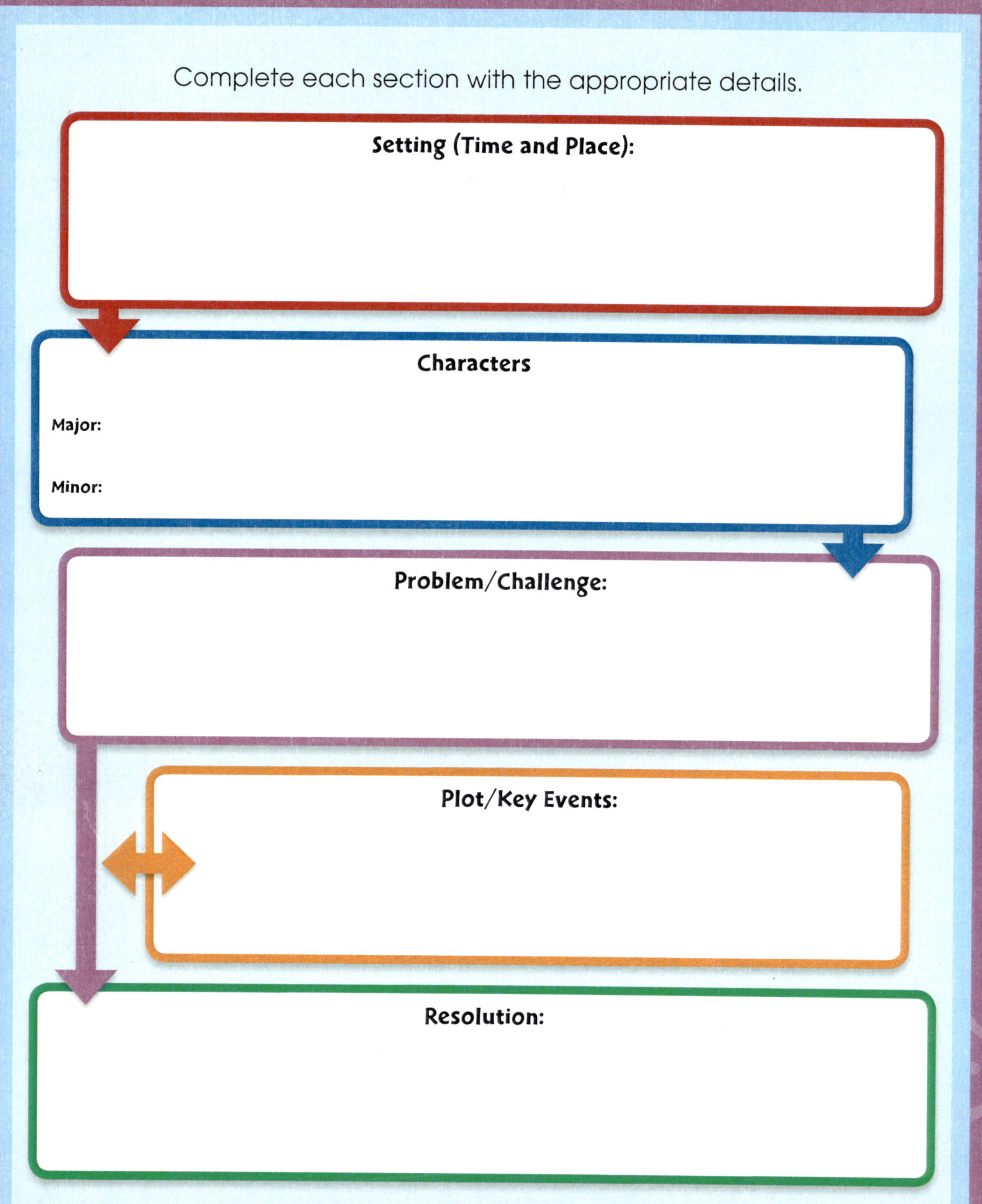